# Good AND Healthy COOKING

D0942980

*Recipes and wisdom from a Mother's heart on how to cook healthy yet simple meals.*

For additional copies contact:

Amanda and Marie Stoltzfus
145 Reading Road | East Earl, PA 17519
717-413-4994
goodandhealthycooking@gmail.com
GoodandHealthyCooking.com

ISBN Spiral Bound: 978-0-692-27246-6

Layout & Design | Valerie Miller
Photography | Alan Homersly

Carlisle Printing
OF WALNUT CREEK LTD
800.927.4196 · carlisleprinting.com
Sugarcreek, Ohio 44681

# Acknowledgments

I found myself humbled by the grace and generosity of friends supporting me in this project. Your interest was a tremendous encouragement to me.

I especially thank the Fisher sisters, Linda, Verna, and Anna, for your perseverance in helping to prepare all the recipes for photos. I look back on all those times with fondness, and laugh as I remember the funny moments!

And a special thank you to the Homersly's. Alan, this project is richer because of your commitment and dedication to the best pictures possible. Your photography has exceeded my wildest imaginations and expectations! And Jill, you have been the glue holding the chaos together when dishes piled up, time was running out, and when something ' just wasn't quite right' about that picture. Thank you for quietly and patiently picking up those loose ends. Oliver, what a blessing to watch you working, playing, and being a part of our family.

Thanks to all of you at Carlisle Printing. We've been so blessed to be working with you. From that first meeting its been so much more than business, it has been friendship.

And the biggest thank you of all, to my family! I know it was hard to wait to eat until we had that picture "just perfect". You've all very much been a part of the months it has taken in creating this book, and I have been thankful and encouraged by your interest. Ephraim, my sweetheart, I could never have done this without you believing in me and encouraging me to follow my dream. You've been an encouragement, inspiration, and a stability. I cherish your love and acceptance.

Most of all, I thank Jesus my Redeemer. You have done far beyond what healthy foods could ever do for me. You have given me new life. You have given healing, acceptance, and forgiveness. And you're making a far better home for us that we can ever imagine having here.

*Amanda*

# Table of Contents

# Proverbs 31

1 The words of king Lemuel, the prophecy that his mother taught him.

2 What, my son? and what, the son of my womb? and what, the son of my vows?

3 Give not thy strength unto women, nor thy ways to that which destroyeth kings.

4 It is not for kings, O Lemuel, it is not for kings to drink wine; nor for princes strong drink:

5 Lest they drink, and forget the law, and pervert the judgment of any of the afflicted.

6 Give strong drink unto him that is ready to perish, and wine unto those that be of heavy hearts.

7 Let him drink, and forget his poverty, and remember his misery no more.

8 Open thy mouth for the dumb in the cause of all such as are appointed to destruction.

9 Open thy mouth, judge righteously, and plead the cause of the poor and needy.

10 Who can find a virtuous woman? for her price is far above rubies.

11 The heart of her husband doth safely trust in her, so that he shall have no need of spoil.

12 She will do him good and not evil all the days of her life.

13 She seeketh wool, and flax, and worketh willingly with her hands.

14 She is like the merchants' ships; she bringeth her food from afar.

15 She riseth also while it is yet night, and giveth meat to her household, and a portion to her maidens.

16 She considereth a field, and buyeth it: with the fruit of her hands she planteth a vineyard.

17 She girdeth her loins with strength, and strengtheneth her arms.

18 She perceiveth that her merchandise is good: her candle goeth not out by night.

19 She layeth her hands to the spindle, and her hands hold the distaff.

20 She stretcheth out her hand to the poor; yea, she reacheth forth her hands to the needy.

21 She is not afraid of the snow for her household: for all her household are clothed with scarlet.

22 She maketh herself coverings of tapestry; her clothing is silk and purple.

23 Her husband is known in the gates, when he sitteth among the elders of the land.

24 She maketh fine linen, and selleth it; and delivereth girdles unto the merchant.

25 Strength and honour are her clothing; and she shall rejoice in time to come.

26 She openeth her mouth with wisdom; and in her tongue is the law of kindness.

27 She looketh well to the ways of her household, and eateth not the bread of idleness.

28 Her children arise up, and call her blessed; her husband also, and he praiseth her.

29 Many daughters have done virtuously, but thou excellest them all.

30 Favour is deceitful, and beauty is vain: but a woman that feareth the Lord, she shall be praised.

31 Give her of the fruit of her hands; and let her own works praise her in the gates.

Making Healthy Choices

# Stepping Into Health

**First Steps**

It all started back when I was a young bride. I learned that my new husband appreciated the taste of whole wheat. Eager to please him, I experimented by using half whole wheat instead of white flour. While my husband loved it, I had a rather hard time adjusting to the taste. I know now that freshly-ground wheat tastes so much better!

We can all start somewhere! It is my goal to inspire you to take that first step in Good and Healthy Cooking, and to start wherever is best for your family.

**Bigger Steps**

My next step was to avoid white sugar. Because of a lot of health issues, I continued researching nutrition and developed a huge interest in healthy foods. I suffered from autoimmune issues and rheumatoid arthritis and was told by a doctor that I could be in a wheelchair by the time I turned thirty.

And then, we received the earth-shattering news that our daughter Marie was diagnosed with leukemia. Desperate to help her recover and to off-set the side effects of chemotherapy, we consistently focused on a diet high in fats and low in carbs. We gave her plenty of grass-fed meats, raw Jersey milk, butter, cream, coconut oil, healthy fats and proteins.

The results? After the initial diagnosis, Marie no longer needed hospital stays or emergency visits during her two years and three months of treatment. Her medication was reduced. She amazed her doctors with her resilience and quick recovery. Of course, there were so many people praying for her as well, so we cannot say it was all food related.

One of the easiest changes toward healthy homemaking is switching to healthy fats. When I don't eat enough healthy fats my bones ache, my appetite is not satisfied and my energy is lower. Another super-easy and healthy change is to switch to using a healthy, unrefined salt.

Amazingly enough, to this day I have no trace of rheumatoid arthritis. That is enough to convince me to keep up those healthy fats.

# Stepping Into Health

## Stepping Joyfully

Whatever steps we are taking toward healthy homemaking, we homemakers do need to keep in mind that healthy foods do not make a happy home. Our children and husband thrive in a home where mother is cheerful and laughing, not stressed when she occasionally needs to serve foods that don't meet her 'healthy' standard because of lack of time and energy. Joy can boost our health as much as healthy foods, while heaviness and stress can cause sickness and diseases. The Bible says that bitterness is as rottenness in the bones. Repenting of bitterness in my life was a huge part of healing my body from rheumatoid arthritis.

## Family Steps

In my home I want healthy cooking to be a family interest. Healthy foods can taste so good! And since first impressions are often lasting impressions, I try to make it taste especially good when I serve it the first time. Putting it in a pretty dish helps too.

When my children help me prepare a meal, they are so much more apt to enjoy the food, especially when we all make a big deal out of thanking them for the meal!

When I plan ahead and don't rush through meal preparation, I can enjoy having my little ones helping me.

Putting a meal on the table is so much more than food. It is togetherness in serving others. It is fellowship with those we love. It is HOME.

Making Healthy Choices

3

# Making Healthy Choices

## Hydrogenated Oils

For a while I was confused with all the different names of fats and oils. I knew our bodies needed healthy fats, but were trans-fats good or bad? Expeller-pressed was good, but what was a hexane-expressed oil? Somehow that didn't sound as good!

It doesn't need to be confusing and we do not need to remain uninformed. I find it easier to stay away from foods that are unhealthy when I understand why they are bad for me.

Simply put, hydrogenated oil is a liquid oil changed into a solid or partly solid state through hydrogenation, like margarine or shortening. This usually involves heating to an incredibly high heat, up to 1000°, and then injecting with metal such as nickel, platinum or aluminum. Before hydrogenation, these oils are unsaturated fats in their natural state. After hydrogenation, these oils become trans fats. These oils are really more like plastic than food.

These oils are seriously detrimental to our family's health and energy levels. They cause the blood to thicken causing the heart to work much harder to pump the blood throughout the system, thus contributing to high blood pressure, high cholesterol and heart attacks. Hydrogenated oils can slow the circulation to the brain, thus causing various emotional and physical ailments. They wreak havoc on your immune system and cause cancers, diabetes, increase asthma and reduce fertility.

The body never really succeeds in digesting these plastic-like oils, neither was it made to! These oils are not really food anymore.

A few other names for hydrogenated oils could be shortening, partially hydrogenated oil and trans-fats. Hydrogenation is used for cooking oils, including canola, cottonseed, vegetable, corn and many others. Basically, any oil that isn't cold-pressed or centrifuge extracted.

## Unrefined Fats and Oils

Did you know that your brain must have healthy fats to function properly and to be strong?

# Making Healthy Choices

Now, not just any fats will do. Your brain needs saturated fats like butter, cream, coconut oil and red meats. Saturated fats make us feel satisfied so I call them the 'Satisfying Saturates'! This satisfied feeling reduces food cravings. Take a look at the oils in my kitchen and why we use these.

**Butter-(Grass Fed)** builds the immune system, supports the heart, helps the bones build calcium and has strong cancer-fighting properties.

**Coconut Oil-(Centrifuged or Cold-pressed)** has anti-fungal and anti-microbial properties, so it protects your body from bacteria and fungus, builds your immune system and prevents intestinal disorders. Plus coconut oil stabilizes weight and aids in weight loss.

**Extra Virgin Olive Oil-(Cold-Pressed)** fights inflammation and lowers blood pressure.

**Palm Shortening (Cold Pressed)** These fats are great for high-heat frying. Try making French fries or potato wedges in Palm Shortening.

## Eating White Sugar and Flour

Eating white sugar and white flour forces a release of your brain's 'feel good' neurotransmitters, serotonin, and endorphins. What this means is that white sugar and white flour make you feel good, but only for a short time. Guess what happens next? After the feel good is all used up you feel bad, not good! That's because your body has used up all those feel-good neurotransmitters.

But wait! Your brain has the solution: Eat another cookie and get more feel good! This sugar will release more of your brain's feel-good neurotransmitters.

So… you grab another cookie… and another… and another… until those feel goods are all used up and you are like a car trying to run on empty! There are simply no feel goods left, and no energy.

By avoiding so much white sugar and white flour your body can produce a full tank of those neurotransmitters without wasting them, thus releasing them naturally. If you suffer from depression you might find it helpful to avoid white sugar and white flour.

Making Healthy Choices

5

# Making Healthy Choices

## High Fructose Corn Syrup

When we go shopping I have a list of ingredients that I teach my children to avoid. My oldest two have this list pretty well memorized. On the top of this list is high fructose corn syrup. We check the ingredients and if the product contains HFCS it usually goes right back on the shelf. Why? For one thing, high fructose corn syrup is highly addictive, it makes my children very hyper-active, and makes us unable to process emotion, causes memory loss, and helps people gain fat, especially around the middle.

Some suspect that the obesity epidemic in our country is directly linked to using so much high fructose corn syrup. What do you think?

There are very few packaged foods that do not contain high fructose corn syrup, and your body can easily reach toxic levels by dealing with this amount of sugar.

The best way to avoid fake food is to eat real food. Let's make our own.

## MSG Monosodium Glutamate

Glutamates are amino acids that naturally occur in the body. They control some of the functions in the brain, nervous system, eyes and more. But when we add glutamate to our food it puts our body out of balance, our bodies can't deal with this. Then what? It overexcites the cells and can cause nerve damage, irregular heartbeat, skin rashes and difficulty breathing.

MSG encourages our body to overeat.

MSG is a flavor enhancer. It sends pleasure to the brain and gives the feeling of a savory flavor. The brain tells the body it is delicious and nutritious! MSG products create cravings and feel addictive. Now you can see why manufacturers like to use this product. Because of MSG they can use cheaper food products such as wood pulp (cellulose) and TVP (textured vegetable protein).

MSG is found in spices and in processed, packaged and canned foods. It is not always listed as MSG in the ingredients. Hydrolyzed vegetable protein may contain up to 20% MSG and does not

# Making Healthy Choices

need to be listed. Besides this, hydrolyzed vegetable protein may be listed as natural flavors! And there are more than 40 other commercially produced glutamates that function similarly to MSG. Avoid ingredients with words such as 'hydrolyzed,' 'yeast extract,' 'glutamaic acid,' 'isolated protein,' or 'natural flavors.' This is not an exhaustive list. There are many other labels MSG and similar products can hide under. Lets do what we can, taking one step at a time, and provide our families with health-filled, nourishing foods the way God intended them.

## Natural Sweeteners

There are many options available to those of us looking to avoid white sugar and its side effects. Unfortunately, they do cost more, and the more unrefined we seek for, the more money we spend. However, removing sugar from our pantry has had so many benefits, resulting in more energy, better moods, stronger immune system, and less food cravings.

Marie and I really, really like sweets! When I first started using unrefined sugars I thought this meant I could now eat all the sweets and desserts I wanted! But I soon discovered that even healthy sweeteners need to be used in moderation. While these natural sweeteners contain many important vitamins and minerals, truth is most of us could do with less sweets and carbs. Those who have low blood sugar or diabetes will need to limit all sweetener intake very strictly, with the exception of stevia.

If you are struggling with carb and sugar cravings, here is a secret for you: If you eat more healthy fats the cravings will disappear!

My favorite sweetener is raw honey. If it is raw it contains lots of beneficial bacteria and enzymes. Heating destroys these enzymes, so it's best to use other options for baking. You may find that I made an occasional exception in these recipes but only because it resulted in a superior product for that specific recipe.

Coconut sugar is fairly new to me. I use it similarly to sucanat.

Sucanat: Sugar Cane Natural. I prefer to use sucanat or rapadura that is pure, dried sugar cane juice with the vitamins and

# Making Healthy Choices

minerals still intact, nothing removed or added back in.

Maple syrup imparts a wonderful flavor to baked goods. If you substitute another sugar for maple syrup, you may need to add slightly more liquid.

Stevia might take a little experimenting, but don't let that intimidate you! I use it in drinks, teas and yogurt. By adding some to baked goods I can reduce the sugar. The number one rule in using stevia is: don't use too much!

We limit fruit juices to special occasions. Fruit juices, even without added sugars, are too concentrated in fruit sugars.

You will find that you can use even less sugar than what I have in my recipes as you get used to it. The less sugar the sweeter your mood!

## Whole Grain

Whole grains provide lots of B vitamins, vitamin E and many important minerals. But these are destroyed during the commercial refining process. Fiber is also removed. The synthetic vitamins and minerals added to white flour in no way come close to the way God made grains in the first place.

When grains are freshly ground at home they still retain phytase, the enzyme that helps break down phytic acid. Soaking or sprouting further breaks down the phytic acid! Grinding your own flour and using it fresh retains the vitamin content of the grain, plus you have rancid-free flour.

# Making Healthy Choices

## Why We Use Raw Milk?

Raw milk is a living food. It's full of enzymes, beneficial bacteria and vitamins. By pasteurizing the milk, these bacteria and enzymes are destroyed and the milk is hard to digest. Perhaps this is why so many people have digestive issues. In fact, a large percentage of those who cannot tolerate milk are able to use raw milk. Pasteurization involves heating the cold milk extremely fast to 161° (in a few seconds) and then ultra-pasteurizing even higher to 280° F (for one second,) leaving the enzymes and good bacteria completely destroyed. This leaves the milk a dead food rather than living food to nourish your body. However, I recognize that using raw milk is such a controversial subject that only you can make the choice to embrace or decline. Be wise and research the risks and benefits. Do keep in mind that cows grazing on pasture with room to roam will be much healthier and disease-resistant.

## Budget Discovery

Try making your own salad dressings. You can use very healthy ingredients for about the same price as bottled dressings. What an advantage, considering all the additives, rancid vegetable oils and preservatives. You can make a delicious dressing in a few minutes, in almost less time than it would take you to find the salad dressing aisle in the supermarket!

## Time Saver

Each week, sit down and plan your meals and grocery list for the week. This prevents the stress of trying to thaw the dinner at 4:30! It also ensures a balanced, healthy meal. Each evening you can pull the next day's supplies out of the freezer, and stick them in the fridge. For myself, it often goes into the Crockpot the next day.

Making Healthy Choices

# Making Healthy Choices

## An Astounding Discovery

We have found, on our journey toward a healthier diet, that we are actually saving money, although we spend double, or even triple on healthy oils such as extra virgin olive oil, coconut oil, palm oil, etc. versus the common processed vegetable oil. Although we spend more on good quality dairy products, meats and eggs, somehow it comes to a cheaper balance in the end. We have noticed that we are satisfied with less when eating wholesome foods and so with the cheaper, processed foods you end up buying more. And of course it's cheaper to make your own than to buy packaged pastries and cereals.

We hardly ever buy boxed breakfast cereals. They are expensive, difficult to digest and poor in nutrients, even if they are made of whole grains. The same amount of the best quality organic oatmeal costs only half as much and is much healthier. If possible I soak the oatmeal overnight to aid digestion.

## Quality Foods

Don't be too conscious of saving money on good quality foods. That is one of the necessities. Rather, cut out all junk food such as fast foods, soft drinks, chips, pretzels, crackers, packaged pastries and restaurant bills. Use the money you save for good quality wholesome foods. Most importantly, use good quality, satisfying fats.

## Salts

Ye are the Salt of the earth... Matthew 5:13

Hmm... sounds like salt is a good thing, doesn't it? Actually, it is, the way God made it! When salt is in its unrefined, unprocessed state, it is full of amazing vitamins and minerals. God made our bodies to crave salt and its minerals.

When salt is taken through a refining process, chemicals are added to remove the minerals. Without the minerals it looks whiter and cleaner, and assures a longer shelf life. Without these life-giving minerals, the body starts to break down, the immune system suffers, the kidneys are affected, thus causing swelling and high blood pressure. So that's why we use unrefined salts... we can't afford not to!

# Making Healthy Choices

# Making Healthy Choices

# Breakfast

# Pecan Maple Butter

½ cup coconut oil, softened

½ cup butter, softened

1 cup maple syrup

1 cup pecans, coarsely chopped

Mix well with whisk until lumps are gone. If the oil is melted you will need to stir occasionally as it cools so it doesn't separate.

## Variations:

– Omit pecans for maple butter.

– For peanut butter spread omit pecans and add 2 cups peanut butter. Mix well.

– Use fruit pie filling on page 152 for syrup and top with whipped cream.

The name of the LORD is a strong tower;
THE RIGHTEOUS RUN TO IT AND ARE SAFE.

Proverbs 18:10

# Breakfast Pizza

Pizza or Bread dough

1 pound nitrate-free bacon, ham or sausage, cooked

2 cups cooked and shredded potatoes

1 cup shredded cheese

6 eggs, beaten

½ teaspoon salt

⅛ teaspoon black pepper

Roll pizza dough thin in a large 11"x17" pan, or use two smaller round pans. I use refrigerated leftover bread dough from day before. I like to use my cast iron skillets. Spread bacon, ham or sausage on crust. Top with potatoes, cheese, eggs, salt and black pepper. Top with more cheese if desired. Bake uncovered at 375° for 25 minutes. If you bake it in cast iron you may need to bake about 10 minutes longer.

Verily, verily, I say unto you, He that heareth my word, and

*believeth on him that sent me, hath everlasting life,*

AND SHALL NOT COME INTO CONDEMNATION;

but is passed from death unto life.

*John 5:24*

# Hash Brown Breakfast Casserole

2 lbs. raw potatoes, shredded finely

2 teaspoons salt

1 lb. bacon, fried and crumbled

1 onion, diced and finely chopped

1 bell pepper, chopped

12 eggs, beaten

2 cups shredded cheese

½ cup sour cream

2 cloves garlic, chopped

½ teaspoon black pepper

Put in a baking dish and bake, covered, at 350° for 1 hour.

Or put in a well-greased slow cooker & cook on high 3-4 hours or on low for 6-8 hours.

My defence is of God,
*which saveth the upright in heart.*

*Psalm 7:10*

Breakfast

19

# Caramelized Apple Porridge

8–10 apples, peeled, cored and cut into

1" pieces

¾ cup maple syrup

      or less, then add stevia

1 teaspoon salt

2 Tablespoons cinnamon

juice of one lemon

4 cups quick oats

5 cups water

4 cups milk

2 eggs, beaten

Cut apples into 1" pieces. Combine first seven ingredients. Bring to a boil and simmer 5 minutes. Add milk and eggs. Heat until almost boiling. Turn heat off and let the oatmeal sit for 15 minutes. It is ready when the apples are soft and the liquid is absorbed. Gently cook some more if it is still too runny. Add more milk if it gets too thick. Serve with raisins and cinnamon.

*Note: I like to soak the oatmeal overnight in 5 cups water and a teaspoon vinegar. This helps digestion.*

These things have I written unto you that believe on the name of the Son of God;

THAT YE MAY KNOW THAT YE HAVE ETERNAL LIFE,

and that ye may believe on the name of the Son of God.

1 John 5:13

# Breakfast Bread Casserole

12–14 slices bread

1 $\frac{1}{2}$ cups nitrate-free ham or sausage, cooked

2 $\frac{1}{2}$ cups shredded cheese

6 eggs, beaten

3 cups milk

$\frac{1}{2}$ teaspoon ground mustard

$\frac{1}{2}$ teaspoon salt

$\frac{1}{4}$ teaspoon onion powder

$\frac{1}{2}$ cup butter

In a 9″x13″ pan place one layer of bread, ham and cheese, then repeat the layers. Combine eggs, milk and seasonings; pour over bread layers. Add more cheese and meat on top if desired. Cut butter over top. Cover with foil and bake at 375° for 45 minutes. Remove cover, then bake another 10 minutes.

Note: This should be prepared the night before and refrigerated.

For whosoever shall call upon the name of the

Lord shall be saved.

Romans 10:13

# Baked Oatmeal

¼ cup milk

½ cup butter, melted or softened

3 cups oatmeal

1 teaspoon salt

1 Tablespoon cinnamon

½ teaspoon stevia

2 eggs

½ cup maple syrup or honey (or less)

2 teaspoons baking powder

1 teaspoon vanilla

Preheat oven to 350°. Mix in order given. Bake in an 8"x8" pan about 25 minutes or until nicely browned.

*Variations:*

– *Add raisins, nuts, fruit, dried fruit, blueberries, etc.*

– *Sprinkle cinnamon on top.*

– *For peanut butter baked oatmeal decrease butter to ¼ cup, then add ½ cup peanut butter.*

– *For Baked Oatmeal Crumbles, stir halfway through baking.*

24

*And this is the record,*

that God hath given to us eternal life,

**and this life is in his Son.**

1 John 5:11

# Syrupy Pancake Bake

1 egg

1 cup milk or buttermilk

½ teaspoon salt

2 Tablespoons butter or oil

1 cup fresh ground flour

1 teaspoon baking powder

Preheat oven to 350°. In oven, Melt ½ cup butter in the bottom of a 9"x13" pan. After it's melted mix it with ½ cup sucanat. Spread this evenly over the bottom of pan, then pour the batter over top. Bake 20 minutes. To serve: turn it upside down on a platter.

*Notes: I have made this countless times in the last twelve years for an easy quick breakfast when we have guests or for a treat for our family.*

**Variations:**

*— Instead of butter and sucanat you can use 1 cup or more maple syrup to cover the bottom of the pan, then pour the batter over top.*

*— Toss some blueberries or other fruit on top of the batter before baking.*

*- Add nuts to syrup, then pour batter on top.*

For God so loved the world, that he gave his only begotten Son,

*that whosoever believeth in him should not perish,*

BUT HAVE EVERLASTING LIFE.

John 3:16

27

# French Toast Casserole

1 cup maple syrup

10–16 slices bread

5 eggs

1 teaspoon vanilla

1½ cups milk

¼ teaspoon salt

Pour maple syrup into 9″x13″ cake pan. Lay the bread on top. Mix the eggs, vanilla, milk and salt, and gently pour over the bread. Refrigerate overnight. Bake, covered at 350° for 40–45 minutes.

He that hath the Son hath life; and
*he that hath not the Son of God hath not life.*

1 John 5:12

Breakfast

# Sausage Breakfast Pie

1½ cup sausage, cooked, either ground
or sliced

3 eggs

¾ cup fresh ground flour

½ teaspoon salt

½ teaspoon pepper

1½ cup milk

2 Tablespoons butter

Cheese if desired

Put sausage in bottom of casserole. Mix together rest of ingredients. Pour over sausage crust. Bake, uncovered at 350° for 25–30 minutes.

*And hereby we do know that we know him,*

IF WE KEEP HIS COMMANDMENTS.

1 John 2:3

# Whole Wheat Pancakes

3 eggs

3 cups whole milk, buttermilk,
   or sour milk

1 ½ teaspoon salt

2 ¼ cups fresh ground flour

3 teaspoons baking powder


Whisk well, fry on a well-buttered skillet.


**Variations:**

*- For lighter, fluffier pancakes separate the egg yolks, and beat the egg whites until fluffy. Add these last, mixing gently.*

*- Use Cream or sour cream.*

And I give unto them eternal life; and they shall never perish,
*neither shall any man pluck them out of my hand.*
John 10:28

# The Best Waffles

1½ cups fresh ground flour, sifted

1½ teaspoons baking powder

½ teaspoon baking soda

1 Tablespoon sucanat, honey, or maple syrup

3 eggs yolk, save egg whites

1½ cups cream

½ cup butter, melted

1 teaspoon salt

1 teaspoon vanilla

Mix well. In a separate bowl, beat the 3 egg whites until stiff. Gently fold this into the batter.

Now to use the waffle iron:

1. Have the waffle iron very hot before you pour the batter on.

2. Always grease the waffle iron very well. You can use a cooking spray or brush the butter or coconut oil on. Use plenty.

3. Don't overfill. Follow your waffles iron's instructions.

4. I cook them for almost 1 minute per side.

You will keep in perfect peace him

*whose mind is steadfast, because he trusts in you.*

Isaiah 26:3

# Blueberry Muffins

2 eggs

¾ cup maple syrup

⅓ cup butter, melted

⅓ cup milk or cream

1 teaspoon vanilla

1 teaspoon lemon juice

1 ½ cups fresh ground flour

½ teaspoon salt

2 teaspoons baking powder

1 ½ cups blueberries

Mix in order given. After mixing carefully fold in blueberries. Do not stir the blueberries too much or your batter will turn blue. Gently fold them in. Butter your muffin cups very well or line them with cupcake papers. Fill muffin cups about ¾ full. Bake at 400° for 15 minutes or until a toothpick inserted in center comes out clean. Yield: 12 muffins

*Tip: if you want more fruit in your muffins add some dried blueberries.*

**Variations:**

– *For Apple Cinnamon Muffins, peel and dice 1 ½ cups apples and add 1 teaspoon cinnamon. Add raisins if desired.*

– *Use dried strawberries or other dried fruit and nuts if desired.*

– *Use fresh peaches.*

*It is God that girdeth me with strength,*

and maketh my way perfect

Psalm 18:32

# Granola

10 cups oats

4 cups fresh ground flour

2 cups honey

1 teaspoon salt

4 teaspoon cinnamon

½ teaspoon stevia

1 teaspoon vanilla

1 cup coconut oil, melted, or add butter

1 cup butter, melted

½ cup milk

Preheat oven to 250°. Mix ingredients together. Spread on cookie sheets. Bake about 1 hour; stirring every 15 minutes until golden brown and crunchy. After baking add sunflower seeds, coarsely chopped nuts, peanut butter, raisins, craisins, dried fruits, chia seeds, or even cocoa powder for chocolate granola.

Cool before adding dried fruit, but add peanut butter and cocoa right away.

FOR BY GRACE ARE YE SAVED THROUGH FAITH;
*and that not of yourselves: it is the gift of God:*
Ephesians 2:8

# Farmer's Breakfast

¼ cup butter

2 cups cubed small potatoes

¼ cup chopped bell peppers

½ cup chopped onions

¾ teaspoon salt

¼ teaspoon black pepper

6–8 eggs, beaten

2 Tablespoons milk or cream

1 cup nitrate-free ham or sausage, diced

1 cup shredded cheese

Melt butter in skillet. Add potatoes, peppers, onions, salt and pepper. Cook over medium heat until potatoes are soft. Pour eggs, milk or cream, and ham or sausage over potatoes. Cook, stirring gently until eggs are done. Don't overcook. Add shredded cheese.

**Variations:**

– You can use this as a filling for breakfast burritos.

# Glazed Cinnamon Biscuits

**2 cups fresh ground flour**

**2 teaspoons baking powder**

**½ teaspoon salt**

**½ cup butter, softened or cubed**

**¾ cup buttermilk or whole milk**

**3 Tablespoons cinnamon**

**½ cup sucanat, coconut sugar or honey**

**¼ cup chopped pecans or walnuts**

**3 Tablespoons butter**

Mix first four ingredients together well; add milk. Mix together well with your hands. Roll the dough onto a floured counter top. Add more flour as needed, roll and pat dough to about ½″ thick. Turn the dough around as you roll, making sure its not sticking to the counter. When your dough is about ½″ thick, spread cinnamon, sugar or honey, and pecans or walnuts over the dough. Fold dough in half, then fold over again. Cut biscuits with biscuit cutter. All the loose dough can be folded into biscuits. Melt three tablespoons butter in your baking dish, then place biscuits in hot baking dish or cast iron skillet. Bake at 425° for 20 minutes. Make a glaze while they bake.

# Glaze

**8 oz. cream cheese, softened**

**¾ cup honey or maple syrup**

Whisk cream cheese and honey, or maple syrup until smooth. Pour over biscuits when done baking. Let sit 5–10 minutes before serving if you can wait that long!

# Grapenut Crunchies

**7 cups fresh ground flour**

**2 cups sucanat**

**2 teaspoons soda**

**1 teaspoon salt**

**3 cups buttermilk or milk**

**½ cup butter, melted**

**1 ½ teaspoons stevia**

Combine well, spread into two cake pans. Bake at 350° for 50 minutes. Cool, then crumble well with your hands, grinder, blender, food processor, or a grater; then spread on two large cookie sheets and bake at 250° for about 45 minutes until well dried. Stir occasionally Cool, then store in a tight container.

*This is our favorite cereal!*

# Homemaker Helps

## Baking Day

One day a week we have baking day. My children range in ages from 2 months–13 years, so our baking efforts can easily become chaotic. With a little forethought though, this can be a very fun and productive time. There are a few ideas that work for us. First, I needed to start small! I have a baking list (shown at right) that I make copies of and check the ones we'll need in the next week. At this point some of the recipes are always made by the same person to avoid the chaos of everyone needing Mom at the same time! For some recipes we work in teams with an older one helping the younger. Depending on the ages of your children you may want to start each person only doing one recipe per baking day until they get used to it. The goal is to have fun working together. My 2-year-old enjoys mixing cakes or cookies. Our Baking Day takes about two hours, plus clean-up. Have fun and don't forget to taste the goodies together.

| name | ✓ | Projects |
|---|---|---|
| Andrew | ✓ | chocolate milk mix syrup |
| Samuel | ✓ | salad dressing |
| Samuel | ✓ | mayonaise |
|  |  | hummus/bean dip |
|  |  | fermented veggies - 1 gallon |
| Marie + Faith | ✓ | mixes: ranch, chili powder, taco seasoning |
| Marie + Faith | ✓ | granola |
|  |  | grapenuts |
| Momma + Jonathan | ✓ | bread |
|  |  | breakfast cakes |
|  |  | pies or pie crusts |
| Samuel + Christopher | ✓ | cakes, |
|  |  | cookies |
|  |  | bars |

*Baking Day Fun!*

# Breads & Salads

# Crescent Rolls

2 Tablespoons yeast

1 ½ cups warm milk or cream, 105–115°

½ cup maple syrup or desired sweetener

½ cup butter

1 egg

1 ½ teaspoons salt

5 cups fresh ground flour

Mix first two ingredients. Let soak 5 minutes then add sweetener, butter, egg and salt. Gradually add flour. Knead well with your hands, adding more flour if it is too sticky. Let rise till double in size. Punch dough down, divide into three balls. Roll each ball into a circle like pizza dough. Melt ¼ cup butter and spread it over the circles. Cut each circle into 12 wedges like cutting a pizza. Roll each wedge up, starting with the outside wider edge and roll in. Place each roll on a baking sheet. Let rise 40 minutes. Bake at 375° for 13–15 minutes until nicely browned.

## Variations:

– You can fill these crescents with yummy fillings. Just add a thin layer of filling after you pour the melted butter over the wedges. Here are some ideas to get your creativity sparked: cheese, chopped peppers, onions, jam, cinnamon, sucanat, spinach, lemon juice, honey or maple syrup, nuts and sucanat, and a dash of cinnamon. Cover with powdered xylitol when baked.

48

# Cheese Wheat Thins

2 cups fresh ground flour

$\frac{1}{4}$ teaspoon soda

1 Tablespoon sucanat or coconut sugar

$\frac{1}{2}$ cup cold butter, cubed

2 teaspoons onion powder

$\frac{1}{2}$ teaspoon salt

$\frac{1}{3}$ cup milk

$\frac{1}{2}$ cup grated cheese, optional

Crumble together first six ingredients. Add milk and cheese. Knead only until smooth. Add slightly more flour if needed. Roll these thinly onto greased baking sheets. Cut into squares with a  pizza cutter; prick each square with a  fork. Bake at 375° for 12–15 minutes.

Not by works of righteousness which we have done,

BUT ACCORDING TO HIS MERCY HE SAVED US, BY THE

*washing of regeneration, and renewing of the Holy Ghost;*

Titus 3:5

# Whole Wheat Bread

3 Tablespoons yeast

4 ½ cups lukewarm water

¾ cup butter, melted or
   extra virgin olive oil, or palm shortening

½ cup sucanat or honey

2 Tablespoons wheat gluten, heaping

1 ½ Tablespoons salt

13–16 cups flour

Mix the yeast and water, set aside for 5 minutes. Then mix butter, sucanat and wheat gluten. Add salt and flour. Add only enough flour till you reach a proper consistency, which means it doesn't stick to your fingers too much. It's also important to knead well while adding flour, and add small amounts of flour towards the end. Cover and let rise 30 minutes or more, then put into bread pans. Make 3–5 loaves, depending on the size of your pans. Let rise until double in size. Bake at 350° for 20–30 minutes.

*Remember with bread making, practice means progress!*

**That if thou shalt confess with thy mouth the Lord Jesus,**

and shalt believe in thine heart that God

hath raised him from the dead, thou shalt be saved.

Romans 10:9

# Breadsticks

1 ½ cups warm water

1 Tablespoon yeast

2 Tablespoons extra virgin olive oil

1 Tablespoon sucanat, maple syrup, or honey

1 ¼ teaspoons salt

4 cups flour

 

Seasoning Mixture:

½ cup butter

3 Tablespoons extra virgin olive oil

1 teaspoon garlic powder

½ teaspoon salt

2 Tablespoons parsley flakes

Mix first two ingredients and set aside for five minutes. Add olive oil, sweetener, salt and flour. Let rise for 1 hour. On a large cookie sheet with sides, roll out this dough. Add more flour if it's too sticky. Set aside.

Seasoning Mixture: In a saucepan melt butter. Add rest of ingredients. Pour this mixture over the dough in the pan. With a pizza cutter, cut the dough into strips. Let this rise until almost double in size. Bake for 15–18 minutes.

# My Favorite Sauerkraut

1 large cabbage, cored and shredded

1 cup grated carrots

2 medium onions, finely chopped, optional

¼–½ teaspoon red pepper flakes

1 Tablespoon caraway seeds

1 Tablespoons unrefined sea salt

4 Tablespoons whey or an additional Tablespoon salt

In a large bowl combine all these ingredients. Mix well and squeeze it with your hands until juices are released. You won't need much juice. Place this in two quart jars and push it down until the juices cover the cabbage. Do not fill the jars to more than an inch from the top. Cover tightly and keep jars at room temperature for about three days, then transfer to cold storage. I like to keep refrigerated at least a week before opening. This will keep a long time. The sauerkraut does get a bit strong after a few months.

**Variations:**

– *For traditional sauerkraut, use only cabbage, salt and whey.*

– *For Kimchi, use 1 head cabbage, 1 cup grated carrots, 1 Tablespoon freshly grated ginger; 3 cloves, garlic peeled and minced, ½ teaspoon red pepper flakes, 1 Tablespoon salt, and 4 Tablespoons whey.*

# Broccoli and Cauliflower Salad

1 large head broccoli, or half broccoli
   and half cauliflower

1 onion, chopped

8–10 nitrate-free bacon, fried and sliced

1 cup homemade mayonnaise
   or sour cream

$\frac{1}{4}$ cup maple syrup or honey

3 Tablespoons vinegar

$\frac{1}{4}$ teaspoon stevia

$\frac{1}{4}$ teaspoon black pepper

Wash and coarsely cut up the broccoli and cauliflower. Set aside. Mix all other ingredients and pour over broccoli and cauliflower. Refrigerate until serving.

*Tip: This salad can be prepared a day or two before serving.*

Examine yourselves, whether ye be in the faith;
prove your own selves. Know ye not your own selves,
how that Jesus Christ is in you, except ye be reprobates.

2 Corinthians 13:5

# Homemade Mayonnaise

2 eggs, pasteurized and fresh

1 teaspoon salt

1 teaspoon dry mustard

½ teaspoon paprika

2 Tablespoons raw apple cider vinegar

2–3 Tablespoons fresh squeezed

    lemon juice

1½–2 cups cold-pressed oil of your choice,

    (I use half coconut oil, melted and half

    extra virgin olive oil)

Combine all ingredients in a blender except the oil. Gradually add oil while blending. The oil should be poured in as thin a line as possible, not just dumped in. You may not need all the oil, but add it until you have a mayonnaise consistency. You may want to add herbs and spices of your choice.

**Variations:**

— *Experiment! I like to add more lemon juice and vinegar after the mayonnaise is done, and turn this into a blender full of salad dressing. I add honey, garlic, onions, fresh oregano and black pepper to taste. Even add some ketchup to make a French Dressing. I love to add pickle juice leftover from a can of homemade pickles. So develop your own unique dressing.*

# Our Family's Salad Dressing

1 medium onion

⅓ cup honey

½ teaspoon salt

½ teaspoon pepper

1 teaspoon celery seed

1 Tablespoons mustard

⅓ cup vinegar

1 cup extra virgin olive oil

2 Tablespoons sour cream or homemade
   mayonnaise, (more if desired)

Blend all the ingredients in a blender and it's ready to serve! Refrigerate leftovers up to a week or longer.

*Variations:*

– *Yummy salad additions: dried cranberries, diced apples and walnuts with a vinaigrette.*

Try healthy alternatives to the bottled salad dressings. Almost all commercial salad dressings are made of dangerously rancid high-temperature oils. Further more, they contain stabilizers, preservatives, artificial flavors and colors, refined sweeteners and neurotoxic MSG. Try a homemade dressing of Extra Virgin Olive Oil with raw vinegar and lemon juice. Good dressings take very little time to make.

# Marie's Famous Cole Slaw

1 head cabbage, cored and shredded

1 cup mayonnaise page 60

   or sour cream

1 lemon, juiced

1 teaspoon salt

$\frac{1}{2}$ teaspoon black pepper

2 Tablespoons vinegar

2 Tablespoons honey or maple syrup


Mix well. Refrigerate.

Whosoever believeth that Jesus is the Christ is born of God:

AND EVERY ONE THAT LOVETH HIM THAT BEGAT

LOVETH HIM ALSO THAT IS BEGOTTEN OF HIM.

1 John 5:1

65

# Biscuits Supreme

**7 cups flour**

**¼ cup sucanat or honey**

**⅓ cup butter**

**3 cups milk**

**2 Tablespoons baking powder**

In a large bowl, using your hands to mix, mix ingredients until blended. Add more flour if this is too sticky. Preheat oven to 400°. With a cookie dipper scoop dough onto greased cookie sheets. Use your hands to form them nicely. Bake for 15  20 minutes or until browned. Dip them into melted butter. These are delicious served with stew instead of crackers.

*Variations:*

*– Add garlic and herbs.*

*– For cheese biscuits add 2 cups shredded cheese.*

# Cornbread

¾ cup cornmeal

2 cups flour

¼ cup maple syrup or honey

¼ teaspoon stevia

3 teaspoons baking powder

½ teaspoon salt

1 cup milk

¾ cup butter, melted

3 eggs, beaten

1½ cups small kernel corn, optional

Mix first six ingredients. Slowly add milk, butter, eggs and corn. Pour into a greased 9"x9" baking dish. Bake at 400° for 20-25 minutes, or until toothpick inserted in center comes out clean.

*Variations:*

*– When you have leftover chili or beans in the fridge, put it in a 9"x13" pan. Mix up this cornbread and pour batter on top of chili. Bake at 400° for 30 minutes until cornbread is done. Serve with sour cream, salsa and a salad. You may need to bake this longer if you add corn.*

Jesus answered and said unto him, Verily, verily, I say unto thee,

## Except a man be born again,

he cannot see the kingdom of God.

John 3:3

# Homemaker Helps

## Packing Lunches

On Mondays my husband works a long day and needs a packed lunch. Because of my lack of preparation, most Monday's find my mind blank and my cupboards bare of any lunch box items, resulting in my husband needing to buy his own lunch.

I've come up with a workable solution. When we have a meal of sandwiches I make a few extra and freeze them for Monday morning lunch boxes, then put fresh lettuce and onions on the side. On baking day I freeze some muffins or cookies.

When I bake bread I often make my very original Stromboli containing leftover meats, shredded cheese, onions, peppers and maybe a little pasta sauce. I wrap leftover pieces and put them in the lunch box section of my freezer. My family enjoys these leftovers even served cold with salsa.

A salad, fruit, or veggie sticks with dip, nicely rounds out this lunch box. I recommend taping a list of lunch box ideas inside your kitchen cupboard doors. Here are some ideas from my list.

## Make a list

Trail Mix: dried fruit and nuts; hard-boiled eggs, peeled and chilled; cheese and homemade crackers; Jell-O made with leftover smoothie; salad or Pasta salad, veggie sticks, egg sandwich, chicken salad sandwich.

## Lots of Lists

I make lots and lots of lists. The inside of my kitchen cupboard doors hold my lists of meal ideas, packed lunch ideas, meal ideas for unexpected guests, plus my bread recipe for easy access and viewing above my mixer. I make lists for Baking Day, Cleaning Day, and, if you don't have a master shopping list I would very highly recommend it. This is a list of all the household items and groceries I buy and where I buy them. On the morning of my shopping I glance over this list and mark what we need. I keep lists of meal ideas to refer to when I plan our menus. Lists are a key to survival for this busy Mom!

# Soups & Sandwiches

# Egg Salad Sandwiches

1 dozen hard-boiled eggs,
  coarsely grated

1 onion, chopped

1 teaspoon salt

1 cup sour cream or plain Greek yogurt,
  or homemade mayonnaise

1 Tablespoon honey or maple syrup,
  optional

¼ teaspoon black pepper

1 teaspoon raw apple cider vinegar or
  some leftover pickle juice

1 Tablespoon mustard

Mix well, then refrigerate until serving.

## Variation:

*– Adding chopped sweet pickles or pickle relish makes it delicious!*

*– How to make perfect, easy to peel, hard-boiled eggs: Cover the eggs with water. Bring to a rolling boil and turn the heat off. In 12 minutes turn the heat back on until boiling. Cool slightly in cold water and peel immediately. Very fresh eggs are hard to peel.*

*– Filled Eggs: Instead of grating the eggs cut them in half lengthwise. Remove the yolks and smash in food processor. Add remaining ingredients. Put this mixture in a plastic bag and snip a little corner off. Squeeze the filling onto the eggs. A bit like using a cake decorator.*

72

Neither is there salvation in any other:
*for there is none other name*
*under heaven given among men,*
**whereby we must be saved.**
Acts 4:12

# Chicken Salad

2½ cups diced cooked chicken

1 stalk celery, chopped

⅓ cup chopped onions

1 teaspoon black pepper

1½ cups sour cream

1 Tablespoon lemon juice or vinegar

Mix all ingredients. Refrigerate. Serve with bread as sandwiches or with crackers.

For the which cause I also suffer these things:
nevertheless I am not ashamed: for I know whom I have believed,
AND AM PERSUADED THAT HE IS ABLE TO KEEP THAT
which I have committed unto him against that day.

2 Timothy 1:12

# Sloppy Joe Sandwiches

1 pound ground beef

1 medium onion, chopped

1 ¾ cups tomato sauce

1 teaspoon salt

½ teaspoon pepper

In a large skillet brown ground beef. Add onion, tomato sauce, salt and pepper. Simmer for 10 minutes. Stir often. Serve on bread with lettuce and shredded cheese if desired.

### Variation:

– *You might like to place sandwiches on a baking sheet and toast in oven for a few minutes. Put lettuce on the side after baking.*

There is therefore now no condemnation to them which are in Christ Jesus, who walk not after the flesh, but after the Spirit.

Romans 8:1

# Blended Soups

I love blended soups. I could probably eat soups every day and never get bored. Plus, they are quick to make and very nourishing! Here are some of my favorites. So get out the blender and sit down to a cozy, comforting meal of blended soup served with crusty bread.

*Carrot Ginger Soup*

**5 large carrots**

**1 cup orange lentils**

**1 onion**

**2 cloves garlic**

**1" piece of ginger, sliced**

**2 cups water**

**2 cups milk or cream**

Cook everything together except milk or cream. After vegetables are softened; add milk or cream and blend. Add salt as needed. Heat again and serve.

*Potato Onion Soup*

**1 pound potatoes**

**1 large onion**

**1 ½ teaspoons salt**

**black pepper**

**1 ½ cups milk or cream**

Cook all together until soft. Add milk or cream, blend, heat and serve.

*Tomato Bisque*

**2 cups blended fresh tomatoes or tomato juice, or diced tomatoes**

**2 cups milk or cream**

**salt**

**pepper**

**1 cup easy melting cheese**

Heat and serve.

*Tip: If you don't have a blender a good quality salsa master may work almost as well. Adding broth makes these soups even more nourishing.*

Soups & Sandwiches

# Cheddar Chowder

2 cups water

2 cups peeled and cubed potatoes

½ cup sliced carrots

½ cup sliced celery

½ cup chopped onions

1 ½ teaspoons salt

¼ teaspoon black pepper

2 cups milk

¼ cup organic cornstarch

¼ cup butter

2 cups shredded cheese

1 cup nitrate-free ham, cooked or another meat

Combine first seven ingredients in 4-quart saucepan. Cover and simmer 10 minutes, then taste to see if vegetables are tender. Mix milk and cornstarch in a separate bowl. When vegetables are tender, gently pour this mixture into soup. Stir. Add butter, cheese and ham. Heat until thick and almost boiling. Serve with breadsticks or biscuits. Yield: 3 quarts

*The Spirit itself beareth witness with our spirit,*
*that we are the children of God:*

Romans 8:16

# Corn Chowder

1 pound loose sausage

1 cup chopped onions

½ cup chopped peppers, if desired

2 cloves garlic, chopped

3 cups corn, fresh or frozen

2 cups milk or cream

½ teaspoon salt

½ teaspoon black pepper

2 Tablespoons flour or organic cornstarch

Brown sausage in stockpot. Add onions,
peppers, garlic and corn. Simmer 10 minutes.
Add milk or cream, salt, black pepper, flour
or cornstarch. Stir as it heats and thickens.
Then serve with bread or crackers.

FOR IF OUR HEART CONDEMN US,
God is greater than our heart,
*and knoweth all things.*

1 John 3:20

# Zucchini Crepes

**1 cup fresh ground flour**

**¾ teaspoon baking powder**

**¾ teaspoon garlic powder**

**dash of salt**

**5 eggs**

**1 cup milk**

**2 cups grated zucchini**

Combine everything except zucchini. Mix. Add zucchini. Fry these on a well-buttered skillet like thin, large pancakes. To serve we set out all the fillings and everyone fills their own crepes, sort of like tortillas. But for your family you may want to assemble all the crepes before the meal. If so, you can hold them together with toothpicks. Prepare all your fillings before frying crepes. Filling ideas: ground beef, fried with barbecue sauce or like sloppy joes, lettuce, tomatoes, shredded cheese, onions, peppers, cucumbers. These are a great variation from regular sandwiches.

### Variation:

— *Try chicken, homemade Ranch dressing, and pineapple.*

85

# Hearty Hamburger Soup

1 large onion, chopped

1½ teaspoons salt

1½ cups water

1 teaspoon garlic powder

½ teaspoon paprika

½ teaspoon black pepper

1 cup sliced carrots

1 cup sliced celery

1 cup cubed potatoes

2 cups tomato sauce

1 pound ground meat, cooked

½ cup organic cornstarch

4 cups milk

Combine the first nine ingredients in a large pot. Simmer until the vegetables are tender. Add tomato sauce, and cooked meat. Mix tapioca starch and milk in separate bowl. Pour this into the soup and stir until it thickens slightly. Serve with bread or crackers.

PEACE I LEAVE WITH YOU; MY PEACE I GIVE YOU. I
DO NOT GIVE TO YOU AS THE WORLD GIVES.
Do not let your hearts be troubled and do not be afraid.

John 14:27

# Homemaker Helps

## Ideas for Leftovers

Cook pasta and mix with leftover chili. Heat thoroughly; top with shredded cheese and serve.

Keep a pan in the freezer and put leftovers in there. After a while the pan will be full and you can put it in the oven for an easy meal.

With our growing family I like to make enough leftovers for another easy meal.

## Encouraging Our Daughters

Keeping the pantry stocked well can greatly stimulate our daughter's creativity in the kitchen. Nothing quite stifles the sudden inspiration to bake like not having the needed ingredients on hand.

Truth be told, sometimes it takes taste buds awhile to get used to the taste of whole grains. One tip: grinding your own flour tastes so much better than the bought whole wheat flour, which turns rancid on the shelves.

Start your meal preparation in plenty of time so the little ones can help you. My goal: To never work alone but make it fun for my children to help me.

## Sensible Savings

Don't waste! Use up leftovers.

Use up what's in your pantry.

Buy less packaged snacks and crackers.

Use rags for spills rather than paper towels.

Make your own spice and seasoning mixes.

Make berry syrups for pancakes instead of maple syrup.

Buy your needed fruits and vegetables in season in large amounts and freeze.

# Main Dishes

# Spanish Rice

1 ½ pounds ground beef or sausage

1 cup uncooked rice

1 Tablespoon salt

2 Tablespoons sucanat

1 quart tomato juice

1 onion, chopped

1 green pepper, chopped

Fry ground beef or sausage. Mix together rest of ingredients and add to meat. Put into a casserole with lid or foil. Bake 1 ½ hours at 350°. This is very hot when it's done. Be careful! Serve with sour cream if desired.

If we confess our sins, he is faithful

and just to forgive us our sins,

AND TO CLEANSE US FROM ALL UNRIGHTEOUSNESS.

1 John 1:9

Main Dishes

# Easy Zucchini Casserole

1 medium sized zucchini,
   finely shredded

1 onion, diced

2 eggs

1 cup bread or leftover toast, diced

1 cup leftover ground beef,
   already cooked

2 Tablespoons butter, cut up

Mix together well, then put in a small baking dish. Bake at 325° for 30 minutes. You may want to double or triple this recipe for large families.

*Variations:*

*– You can use any cooked meat you desire. Adding the broth makes it tasty as well. Sometimes I add cheese.*

# Scalloped Potatoes

8 cups shredded potatoes

2½ cups milk

1 teaspoon salt

1 teaspoon freshly ground flour

2 Tablespoons butter

½ teaspoon black pepper

1 cup shredded cheese, optional

Combine well, then put in a baking dish. Cover, bake for 1 hour at 350°, or until potatoes are tender. Add cheese when finished baking.

Therefore being justified by faith,
we have peace with God through our Lord Jesus Christ:

# Oven Baked Potato Wedges

4 Tablespoons extra virgin olive oil
   or melted butter

4 cloves garlic, sliced or chopped

8 medium potatoes, washed and cut
   into wedges

1 teaspoon salt

1 Tablespoon parsley

Combine ingredients in a large baking dish. Toss. Making sure potatoes are well coated with oil. Lay wedges on side on a cookie sheet. Bake 50 minutes or until wedges are tender and golden. Serve with ketchup if desired.

# Tomato Pie

**Crust:**

2 cups fresh ground flour

2 Tablespoons butter, softened

2 Tablespoons baking powder

1 teaspoon salt

¼ teaspoon oregano

1 egg

1 cup whole milk

**Filling for 2 pies:**

2-3 tomatoes, sliced

2 Tablespoons sucanat

4 slices bread cubed

4 Tablespoons butter

2 cups shredded cheese

dash of garlic powder

dash of black pepper

Mix crust ingredients well then pat into two pie dishes. Slice tomatoes, and put a thick layer on crusts or two thin layers. Sprinkle with sucanat. Cube some bread, and add a layer on tomatoes. Shred cheese and layer some on the bread. Toast two slices of bread, cube it and dip in melted butter. Top your tomato pie with this. Sprinkle garlic powder very lightly on top. Add a shake of black pepper. Bake at 350° for 40 minutes.

JESUS SAITH UNTO HIM, I AM THE WAY, THE TRUTH,
and the life: no man cometh unto the Father, but by me.

John 14:6

# Quiche

9" pie crust, unbaked

1 ½ cups shredded cheese

½ teaspoon salt

¼ teaspoon black pepper

1 Tablespoon onion powder or

    ¼ cup finely-chopped onions

3–4 eggs, beaten gently

1 ½ cups whole milk or cream

Assemble cheese, salt, pepper, onions or onion powder in unbaked pie crust. In another bowl beat together eggs and milk. Pour this over the cheese and crust. Bake for 50–60 minutes or until the center is set. Try some of the delicious variations, and experiment with your own ideas.

## Variations:

– Add basil, dill or garlic powder.

– Add cooked broccoli, asparagus, etc.

– Add chopped spinach.

– Lay some sliced, fresh tomatoes on top and add a dash of basil.

– Here's my favorite variation for the most interesting quiche I have ever had: This one takes a 10" pie crust. Follow all the instructions in the recipe until you come to the eggs. Separate the eggs and set the whites aside. Whisk the egg yolks and the milk. Beat the whites until they're very stiff, then fold them gently into the eggs and milk, don't mix too much. Pour this over the crust and cheese. The egg whites will rise too the top and the crust will be very full. Bake as directed.

He that believeth on the Son hath everlasting life:
and he that believeth not the Son shall not see life;
but the wrath of God abideth on him.

John 3:36

# Creamy White Chicken Chili

1½–2 cups Great Northern beans,
pre-soaked

2½ cups chicken broth

water as needed

1½ teaspoons garlic powder

1 teaspoon salt

1 medium onion, chopped

1 teaspoon ground cumin

1 teaspoon dried oregano

½ teaspoon pepper

¼ teaspoon cayenne pepper

1 pound boneless chicken breasts,
cooked, cut into 1" pieces, or 2 cups
leftover cooked chicken

1 cup sour cream

1 (8 ounce) cream cheese

Combine and cook together Great Northern beans, chicken broth, water, garlic powder, salt, onion, cumin, oregano, pepper and cayenne. When beans are tender add chicken breasts, sour cream and cream cheese. Do not heat too much after adding cream. The beans will need to be cooked on low for

For whatsoever is born of God overcometh the world:
*and this is the victory that overcometh the world, even our faith.*

1 John 5:4

# Stuffing

1 gallon bread cubes

6 eggs

½ teaspoon black pepper

½ teaspoon ground celery seed,
   optional

¾ teaspoon salt

1⅓ pounds butter, melted

8–10 stalks celery, chopped

½ cup chopped onions

Cut bread into small cubes. In a separate bowl mix eggs, pepper, celery seed and salt. Pour over bread cubes. Saute butter, celery and onions. Add to bread. Bake at 300° for 40 minutes, stirring occasionally.

*Variations:*

*– Add cooked and cubed potatoes, carrots or shredded zucchini.*

*For the wages of sin is death; but the gift of God*
is eternal life through Jesus Christ our Lord.

Romans 6:23

# Chili

4 cups kidney beans, cooked

3 pounds ground beef

1 ½ quarts tomato juice

1 cup onions, chopped

½ cup maple syrup, sucanat,
   or coconut sugar

4 Tablespoons chili powder

½ teaspoon black pepper

1 cup chopped green bell peppers

¼ cup vinegar

½ teaspoon dry mustard

4 teaspoons salt

Puree half of beans in the food processor or blender, or just mash them by hand with some of the tomato juice. If chili is too thin add a tablespoon of thickener mixed with ¼ cup water. I use arrowroot, tapioca starch or cornstarch. Repeat this if you want it even thicker.

Study to shew thyself approved unto God,

A WORKMAN THAT NEEDETH NOT TO BE ASHAMED,
rightly dividing the word of truth.

# Easy Tortilla Lasagna

10 tortillas

1 pound ground beef or cubed roast,
   cooked

salt and pepper

1 quart pasta sauce

4 cups grated cheese

Place two tortillas into a lasagna baking
dish. Top with pizza sauce, meat and cheese.
Repeat this process about four times, then
end with tortillas a tiny bit of sauce, and
cheese on top. I like to save a handful of meat
to sprinkle on top. Bake, covered at 350° for
35 minutes. Uncover for the last 5 minutes.

*Variations:*

*– Add cooked black beans to the
meat.*

*– Sometimes I 'hide' beans by
blending them up with sauce.*

*– Add spinach.*

*– Use 2 cups cottage cheese mixed
with 2 eggs. Add some oregano
and garlic powder. You could
then use less grated cheese.*

I am the vine, ye are the branches: He that abideth in me,
and I in him, the same
bringeth forth much fruit:

for without me ye can do nothing.

John 15:5

# Potato Rounds

8 medium potatoes, sliced

1 onion, chopped

½ cup butter, melted

½ teaspoon salt

¼ teaspoon black pepper

¼ teaspoon garlic salt

Mix well, then arrange potatoes neatly in a 9"x13" baking dish. Bake, uncovered at 450° for 30 minutes or until potatoes are tender and golden brown. Yield: 8 servings

**Variation:**

– Add ¼ cup grated Parmesan cheese.

Have not I commanded thee? Be strong and of a good courage;

be not afraid, neither be thou dismayed:

*for the Lord thy God is with thee whithersoever thou goest.*

Joshua 1:9

# Quick Chicken Pie

4 cups cooked and coarsely cut chicken

1 cup chopped carrots

1 cup chopped celery, or peas

1 cup cubed potatoes

¼ cup chopped onions

2 cups milk, divided

3 Tablespoons butter

3 Tablespoons flour

2 cups chicken broth

2 cups fresh ground flour

2 teaspoons baking powder

2 teaspoons butter, cubed

1 teaspoon salt

1 egg

Lay first five ingredients in a baking dish or two large pans. In a saucepan mix 1 cup milk, butter, flour and chicken broth. Cook this until boiling, stirring often, then pour over veggies. In another bowl mix rest of ingredients. Pat or drop this topping batter over chicken pies. Bake at 350° for 30 minutes.

*The angel of the Lord encampeth round about them that fear him, and delivereth them.*

Psalm 34:7

# Skillet Grilled Chicken

4 boneless, skinless chicken breasts,

   cut in strips

1 teaspoon salt

1 teaspoon garlic powder

1 teaspoon onion powder

$\frac{1}{2}$ teaspoon black pepper

$\frac{1}{2}$ teaspoon dried oregano

Heat skillets and melt a tablespoon of butter in each. Place chicken breasts in hot skillet. Sprinkle with rest of ingredients. Cover and grill the chicken 8 minutes on each side on very hot skillet.

But seek ye first the kingdom of God,
*and his righteousness; and all these things*
*shall be added unto you.*

Matthew 6:33

# Easy Baked Corn

3 cups corn, frozen from your garden

   works great!

3 eggs

2 Tablespoons butter, cut up

2 Tablespoons Flour

1 cup milk

1 teaspoon salt

½ teaspoon black pepper

Combine all ingredients and put them in a 8x10 casserole. Bake, uncovered at 325° for 50 minutes.

# Oven Fried Chicken Drumsticks

3 Tablespoons unrefined sea salt

1 teaspoon black pepper

1 Tablespoon honey

12 chicken drumsticks

1 cup fresh ground flour

2 teaspoons salt

½ teaspoon cayenne pepper

½ teaspoon paprika

Mix first four ingredients. Marinate in refrigerator at least four hours. Discard marinade and drain chicken on towels. Preheat oven to 350°. Mix rest of ingredients and coat chicken with mixture. Then arrange them on a baking sheet with sides. Bake 45 minutes. Then turn chicken. Increase oven temperature to 425° and bake 15 more minutes.

*For thou, Lord, art good, and ready to forgive;*
and plenteous in mercy
unto all them that call upon thee.

Psalm 86:5

# Delicious Zucchini Pie

bread dough

¼ cup butter

4 cups grated zucchini

1 cup chopped onions

2 Tablespoons parsley

½ teaspoon salt

½ teaspoon black pepper

½ teaspoon garlic powder

½ teaspoon oregano

½ teaspoon basil

2 eggs, beaten

8 ounces cheese, shredded

Roll out bread dough as thin as possible and put in pie pans. Mix next nine ingredients in saucepan. Sauté this for about 10 minutes. Remove from heat; add eggs and cheese. Stir, then pour this into crusts. Cover with foil. Bake immediately at 350° for 30 minutes.

*Tips: Leftovers can be frozen. This is a good recipe to use on bread baking day, but you can also use the crescent rolls or breadsticks dough recipe.*

*Note: You could use the Tomato Pie Crust recipe on page 98 for this recipe instead of bread dough.*

**Variations:**

*– Try using 2 cups broccoli instead of zucchini.*

Thy word is a lamp unto my feet,

*and a light unto my path.*

Psalm 119:105

# Barbecued Meatballs

1 ½ pounds ground beef

1 small onion, chopped

2 slices bread, crumbled or crushed in
    food processor

¼ teaspoon black pepper

1 egg

1 teaspoon salt

3 ½ cups ketchup, divided (I use homemade)

4 Tablespoons sucanat or maple syrup

½ teaspoon dry mustard

½ cup water

Mix first seven ingredients, using ¼ cup ketchup. In another bowl mix rest of ingredients. Form balls from the meat mixture. About golf ball size. Place them in a baking dish and pour sauce over top. Bake 1 hour at 350°, covered.

*Variation: You can use this same recipe to make meatloaf. Bake about 1 ½ hours.*

He that dwelleth in the secret place of the most
*High shall abide under the shadow of the Almighty.*
I will say of the Lord, He is my refuge and my fortress:
*my God; in him will I trust.*

Psalm 91:1-2

# Taco Pie

1 9″ unbaked pie crust

1 pound ground beef

1 cup tomato sauce

2 Tablespoons taco seasoning

1 cup sour cream

1 cup cheese

1 cup tortilla chips, crushed

Brown ground beef in skillet. Add tomato sauce and taco seasoning. Pour this into an unbaked pie crust. Add a layer of sour cream, cheese and crushed tortilla chips.

In my distress I cried unto the Lord,

AND HE HEARD ME.

Psalm 120:1

# Yum Honey Mustard Chicken

2 pounds boneless, skinless
   chicken thighs

$\frac{1}{2}$ cup mustard

$\frac{1}{4}$ cup honey or maple syrup

2 Tablespoons apple cider vinegar

$\frac{1}{4}$ teaspoon salt

$\frac{1}{4}$ teaspoon black pepper

1 Tablespoon organic cornstarch

$\frac{1}{2}$ teaspoon salt

Layer chicken in a baking dish. In a separate
bowl mix together all ingredients except $\frac{1}{2}$
teaspoon salt. Sprinkle salt over chicken.
Pour sauce over chicken and bake, covered
at 450° for 40 minutes.

Fear thou not; for I am with thee: be not dismayed;
FOR I AM THY GOD; I WILL STRENGTHEN THEE; YEA,
I will help thee; yea, I will uphold thee with
*the right hand of my righteousness.*
Isaiah 41:10

Main Dishes

127

# Cheesy Potatoes

8 cups shredded or cubed potatoes

1 onion, chopped

3 Tablespoons butter

1 (8 ounce) cream cheese

1 cup sour cream

1 teaspoon salt

1 cup shredded cheese

In a large bowl combine all ingredients. Place mixture in a baking dish. Cover and bake at 350°for 50–60 minutes until potatoes are soft. Stir once or twice during baking time.

# Creamed Celery

2 cups water

4 cups sliced celery

1 Tablespoon maple syrup

½ teaspoon salt

2 Tablespoons butter

¼ cup rich milk or cream

1 Tablespoon organic cornstarch

1 teaspoon apple cider vinegar

Cook the celery in the water. After the celery is tender mix the remaining ingredients. Heat until it is thick and just barely boiling. Keep stirring as it thickens. This is a very good side dish to serve with stuffing.

Casting all your care upon him;

for he careth for you.

# Crusty Bacon Bean Dip Dish

1 pound bacon, save grease

Crust:

3 cups fresh ground flour

1 teaspoon salt

1 teaspoon baking powder

¾ cup milk or cream

2 eggs

1 teaspoon onion powder

4 Tablespoons bacon grease or butter

Filling:

6 cups Kidney beans, cooked

1 teaspoon salt

2 teaspoons chili powder

1 pint pizza sauce

1 onion, chopped

1 green pepper, chopped

bacon, crumbled (I add grease)

1 cup grated cheese

Fry bacon. Set aside and save grease. Mix crust ingredients and pat into the bottom and sides of a 9"x13" baking dish. Set aside. In another bowl mix all the rest of ingredients except cheese. Pour into crust. Top with cheese. Bake at 350° for 30 minutes. Serve with shredded lettuce, tomatoes, sour cream and salsa.

*Create in me a clean heart, O God;*
and renew a right spirit within me.

Psalm 51:10

# Eggplant Parmesan

2 pounds eggplant, sliced thinly

1 egg, beaten

1 cup bread crumbs

2 cups pizza sauce, divided

shredded parmesan cheese

Place half of eggplant slices on a greased baking sheet and sprinkle with salt and pepper. For the remaining eggplant slices dip one side (or both) in beaten egg, then dip in bread crumbs, and place on another baking sheet. Bake at 400° for 25 minutes. You may need to rotate the well-greased baking sheets halfway through baking time. Remove from oven and put pizza sauce in bottom of baking dish. Place the unbreaded eggplant slices in the sauce. Spread another cup of sauce over slices, then layer the breaded slices on top, breaded side up. Top with shredded cheese and return to oven to bake another 15 minutes or until cheese is beginning to brown and sauce is bubbly. Enjoy!

*Variation:*

*– Zucchini works great too!*

DEPART FROM EVIL, AND DO GOOD;
seek peace, and pursue it.

Psalm 34:14

# Creamy Chicken Lasagna

1 box whole wheat lasagna noodles, 16 oz.

4 Tablespoons butter

1 onion, chopped

½ bell pepper

16 ounces sour cream

1 (8 ounce) cream cheese

3 cups cooked chicken, cut up

1 cup chicken broth

¾ teaspoon salt

½ teaspoon black pepper

3 cups shredded cheese

Cook lasagna noodles following package instructions. Saute butter, onion, and pepper. Add sour cream and cheese. Stir until smooth then add chicken, broth, salt and pepper.

Layer noodles in a large lasagna pan or two small ones. Pour sauce over each layer. In middle layer put half the cheese. Continue the layers, then put cheese on top.

Cover and bake at 350° for 30 minutes. Could also be made in a skillet on stove top and gently simmered.

*Variations:*

*– Add spinach to middle cheese layer.*

MAY THE GOD OF HOPE FILL YOU WITH ALL JOY
AND PEACE AS YOU TRUST IN HIM,
SO THAT YOU MAY OVERFLOW WITH HOPE BY
THE POWER OF THE HOLY SPIRIT.

Romans 15:13

# Homemaker Helps

## An Eternal Investment

I look at all my time spent in the kitchen as an investment in my family's health. And when I take the time to teach and work with my children as I prepare food, I consider this extra time and mess an investment in my next generation's spiritual and physical well-being. Yes, there is a cost in not using commercial sauces and canned fruits, store-bought breads and rolls and such. But to be serving my family and working with my little ones to bring nourishing meals to the table makes it all so worthwhile.

Working with my children is a matter of considering my priorities. Do I see their help only as an inconvenience, or as time invested in a soul for eternity?

## Planning Ahead

I find it doesn't take long to make an extra lasagna when I'm making one for dinner. The time required to cook the pasta, brown the meat, and shred the cheese may be about 20 minute, but it takes only a few minutes more to make enough lasagna for the freezer, not to mention no extra dishes to wash up.

When I shred carrots or cheese and know that I'll need some again a few times in my planned meals for the week, I save time by doing extra and putting them in zip-lock bags in the fridge. When I soak and cook beans I do enough for several meals. I highly recommend having a certain spot in the freezer for these preparations, or having some method of remembering them! Guess why?!

# Desserts and Tasty Treats

# Rice Custard

1½ cups cooked rice

2 cups milk or cream

1 teaspoon vanilla

⅓ cup sweetener, maple syrup or honey

2 eggs, beaten

1 teaspoon cinnamon

½ cup raisins

Mix all ingredients together. Pour into a one-and-a-half-quart casserole. Place casserole in a cake pan and put hot water into the cake pan, about 1" deep. This will make the pudding more custard-like. Bake 30 minutes, then carefully stir. Bake 20 more minutes or until set. Serve hot or cold. This can be a side dish or served as a dessert with cream.

**Variation:**

*- After the crust is chilled sometimes I mash it a bit and mix some whipped cream for a rice pudding.*

And it shall come to pass, that whosoever shall

CALL ON THE NAME OF THE LORD SHALL BE SAVED.

Acts 2:21

# Raisin Crisp Cookies

2 cups butter, softened

2 cups sucanat

5 eggs

1 Tablespoon vanilla

1 teaspoon lemon juice, optional

1 Tablespoon soda

1 teaspoon salt

5 cups fresh ground flour

2 cups raisins or other dried fruit

1 cup nuts, if desired

Cream together butter, sucanat, eggs, vanilla and lemon juice. Add rest of ingredients. Shape into golf ball size balls and flatten slightly. Bake at 350° for 10 minutes. Remove from oven. If they aren't quite done let them on the pan 5 more minutes, then put on cooling rack. Yield: 5–6 dozen

**Variations:**

*– This makes a very good chocolate chip cookie, which I make occasionally as a rare treat.*

Ye that fear the Lord, trust in the Lord:

*he is their help and their shield.*

Psalm 115:11

# Healthy Fudge

1 cup coconut oil

1 cup raw honey

½ cup cocoa powder

½ cup almond or peanut butter

Set the coconut oil out to soften, but not melted. Once it is softened, mix it well with a wire whisk, until all lumps are dissolved. Mix remaining ingredients. Pour into a small approximately 4"x6" pan and chill. Cut into 1" squares. Design your own fudge and candy bars. For a thin sheet of chocolate candy bars spread the mixture into a more shallow pan lined with wax paper. Cut into bars. You might need to freeze to remove it from the pan.

*Note: I prefer to use the coconut oil that doesn't have any coconut flavor. If the coconut oil was liquefied you will need to refrigerate and keep mixing it occasional until ingredients stay blended together.*

**Variation:**

*— Make it unique! You can add your choice of nuts or raisins. I like chia seeds sprinkled on top.*

*Blessed is every one that feareth the Lord;*
that walketh in his ways.
Psalm 128:1

# Peanut Butter Cake

3 eggs

1½ cups applesauce

1 cup maple syrup or honey

½ teaspoon stevia

½ cup milk

1 cup peanut butter

1 teaspoon vanilla

1 teaspoon salt

1 teaspoon baking powder

1 teaspoon baking soda

1¾ cups fresh ground flour

Mix ingredients in order given. Pour into a 9″x13″ pan. Bake at 350° for 25–30 minutes, until toothpick inserted comes out clean.

146

But the Lord is my defence;
and my God is the rock of my refuge.

Psalm 94:22

# Samuel's 5 Ingredient Cookies

3 cups natural peanut butter

1 cup honey

½ cup butter

1 teaspoon salt

3 cups quick oats

Stir all ingredients together, adding quick oats last. Roll into balls and put onto oiled cookie sheet. Flatten with palm or a fork. We like to make cute little cookies with this recipe. Bake at 350° for 8–12 minutes, until golden brown. Let cool on cookie sheet for a few minutes; remove and cool. These cookies can be very crumbly.

*Samuel especially likes this recipe because there are only 5 ingredients to mix up.*

*Humble yourselves in the sight of the Lord,*

AND HE SHALL LIFT YOU UP.

James 4:10

Desserts and Tasty Treats

# Easy Pie Fillings

**4–6 cups berries**

**2 Tablespoons organic cornstarch**

**$\frac{1}{2}$ cup sucanat, coconut sugar or**
   **maple syrup**

**2 Tablespoons lemon juice**

**dash of salt**

**stevia, if desired**


Mix and put in a pie crust, or cook on stove top till it boils for pancake or dessert topping. Great with yogurt or ice cream, or to fill crepes.

And ye shall know the truth,

AND THE TRUTH SHALL MAKE YOU FREE.

John 8:32

# Brownies

1 cup butter, softened

$\frac{2}{3}$ cup extra virgin olive oil

$2\frac{1}{2}$ cups sucanat

6 eggs

2 teaspoons vanilla

$2\frac{3}{4}$ cups fresh ground flour

2 teaspoons baking powder

2 teaspoons salt

$\frac{2}{3}$ cups baking cocoa

Mix first five ingredients in a bowl. Add flour, baking powder, salt and cocoa. Put into a 12"x16" pan and bake at 350° for 20 minutes or less. Insert toothpick to test if done baking. Brownies are done when toothpick comes out clean. Don't over bake.

I will instruct thee and teach thee in the

*way which thou shalt go:*

I WILL GUIDE THEE WITH MINE EYE.

Psalm 32:8

# Apple Crisp

1½–2 quarts apples, peeled, sliced
   and cored

2 teaspoons cinnamon

1 cup oatmeal

1 cup sucanat

1 cup fresh ground flour

½ teaspoon baking powder

⅔ cup butter, cut up

Mix apples and cinnamon. Put into a 9″x13″ cake pan. Crumble together oatmeal, sucanat, flour, baking powder and butter; put on top of the apples and bake in preheated oven at 350° for about 50 minutes, until slightly browned and the apples are soft.

*Variation:*

*– You can use any in season or frozen fruits and berries. I like making strawberry rhubarb crisp.*

*– Another neat idea is to put half of the topping on the bottom of the pan, put pie filling on that, then top with remaining crumbs.*

A new heart also will I give you, and a new spirit will I put within you:

*and I will take away the stony heart out of your flesh,*

AND I WILL GIVE YOU AN HEART OF FLESH.

Ezekiel 36:26

# Delicious Pudding

2 quarts milk

½ teaspoon stevia powder

1½ cups sucanat, divided

½ teaspoon salt

4 eggs

¼ cup flour

¾ cup organic cornstarch

2 teaspoons vanilla

Heat milk, stevia, 1 cup sucanat and salt in a saucepan. In a separate bowl, beat the remaining ½ cup sucanat, eggs, flour and cornstarch. When milk is hot, add remaining ingredients slowly, stir constantly until mixture just begins to boil. Strain if it seems lumpy. Add vanilla. Cool fast. Cover with wax paper while cooling. Keep refrigerated.

*Variations:*

*— For a chocolate pudding add cocoa powder while pudding is hot.*

*— This makes a delicious banana cream pie. Cut up about 2 bananas and line them on a pre-baked pie crust. Spoon chilled pudding over bananas. Top with whipped cream if desired. Garnish with chocolate shavings.*

*— For an especially creamy pudding add whipped cream before serving.*

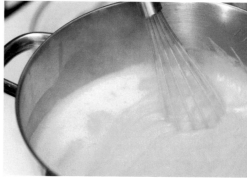

Let your conversation be without covetousness;

nd be content with such things as ye have:

for he hath said, I will never leave thee, nor forsake thee.

Hebrews 13:5

# Fiber Balls

2 cups old-fashioned oats

¾ cup chunky natural peanut butter

½ cup raw honey

¼ cup raisins


Mix, then add more options if desired.


   **Optional Ingredients:**

**wheat germ**

**coconut**

**whole wheat flour**

**sesame seeds**

**almonds**

**chia seeds**

**ground flax seeds**

**currants**


Note: for special treat I add chocolate chips.

For my thoughts are not your thoughts,

NEITHER ARE YOUR WAYS MY WAYS, SAITH THE LORD.

For as the heavens are higher than the earth,

*so are my ways higher than your ways,*

and my thoughts than your thoughts.

Isaiah 55:8-9

# Ginger Cookies

¾ cup butter, softened

1 cup sucanat

1 egg

2 cups fresh ground flour

2 teaspoons soda

2 teaspoons ginger

2 teaspoons cinnamon

¼ teaspoon salt

¼ teaspoon cloves

Mix butter, sucanat and egg. Add rest of ingredients. Cover and refrigerate 1 hour, or until dough is easy to work with. Roll in 1" balls. Bake at 375° for 10–12 minutes until they start to crack on top.

Thou wilt keep him in perfect peace,
whose mind is stayed on thee: because he trusteth in thee.

Isaiah 26:3

Desserts and
Tasty Treats

161

# No Bake Peanut Butter Pie

1 cup heavy cream (sometimes I use
   2 cups for a creamier pie)

1 (8 ounce) cream cheese, softened

1 cup sucanat, maple syrup, or
   coconut sugar

1 cup peanut butter

1 teaspoon vanilla

In a mixer whip heavy cream. Very gently add cream cheese, sweetener, peanut butter and vanilla. In a separate bowl whip 1 cup heavy cream. Gently fold this into peanut butter mixture. Pour into pre-baked pie crust. Refrigerate at least 2 hours before serving.

...for the joy of the

*Lord is your strength.*

Nehemiah 8:10

# Honey Pumpkin Cake

2 eggs

1 cup pumpkin puree

¾ cup honey

½ teaspoon stevia

½ cup butter, softened

½ teaspoon salt

1 teaspoon soda

2 teaspoons baking powder

2 teaspoons cinnamon

1 teaspoon vanilla

½ teaspoon nutmeg

¼ teaspoon ground ginger

¼ teaspoon cloves

⅔ cup water

1½ cup fresh ground flour

Mix ingredients in order given. Pour into a 9"x13" pan and bake at 350° for 25–30 minutes.

*Note: We love having cake and milk for breakfast instead of granola. I do prefer using less sweetener though.*

Be careful for nothing; but in every thing by prayer and supplication
with thanksgiving let your requests be made known unto God.
And the peace of God, which passeth all understanding,
*shall keep your hearts and minds through Christ Jesus.*
Philippians 4:6-7

# Rhubarb Cream Dessert

**Crust:**

½ cup butter, softened

1 cup fresh ground flour

¼ cup sucanat

**Filling:**

3 cups fresh, diced rhubarb

½ cup sucanat

1 Tablespoon flour

**Cream Filling:**

2 (8 ounce) cream cheese

½ cup maple syrup or honey

2 eggs

**Topping:**

1 cup sour cream

2 Tablespoons maple syrup or honey

1 teaspoon vanilla

Press crust ingredients into a 9"x13" pan. Mix filling ingredients and pour over crust. Bake at 375° for 15 minutes. Mix cream filling ingredients together well and pour over rhubarb. Bake again for 30 minutes. After cake is baked immediately pour topping on top. Bake 5 more minutes. Enjoy!

# Frostings for Cakes

*Whipped Cream:*

**1 cup heavy cream**

**1 Tablespoon maple syrup**

Whip heavy cream to the desired consistency, then add maple syrup. You could spread this over the cake, but I like to serve this as a dollop on each individual serving, with a sprinkle of berries or chia seeds. Keep leftovers refrigerated.

*Cream Cheese Icing:*

**1 (8 ounce) cream cheese, softened**

**¼ cup honey or maple syrup**

**whipped cream, optional**

Mix well then spread over cooled cake.

**Variation:**

*– Healthy Fudge page 146 or the No-Bake Peanut Butter Pie page 164 make excellent frostings. But you will have to spread these before they chill in fridge.*

*- Add crushed berries or jam to your favorite frosting.*

168

*The Lord is my light and my salvation; whom shall I fear?*
*the Lord is the strength of my life;*
OF WHOM SHALL I BE AFRAID?

Psalm 27:1

# Orange Poppy Seed Cake

1 cup honey

1½ teaspoon salt

1½ teaspoon vanilla

2 teaspoons almond extract

1 cup butter, melted

3 eggs

1½ cups milk

2½ cups fresh ground flour

1 teaspoon soda

1 teaspoon baking powder

1 teaspoon stevia

2 Tablespoons poppy seeds


Glaze:

¼ cup orange juice concentrate

½ teaspoon stevia

½ cup honey

½ teaspoon vanilla

½ teaspoon almond extract

Mix cake ingredients. Preheat oven to 350°. Pour mixture into a 9"x13" cake pan and bake for 45 minutes. Cool 5 minutes; pour glaze over cake.

*Variations:*

*– For a lemon cake, substitute fresh squeezed lemon juice for the orange juice concentrate.*

*– For Orange Poppy Seed Bread put in two loaf pans.*

God is our refuge and strength,

a very present help in trouble.

Psalm 46:1

# Tiny Keufels

1 cup fresh ground flour

½ cup butter

3 ounces cream cheese


Filling:

1 cup sucanat, or less

1 egg

¼ cup butter, melted

¼ teaspoon salt

1 teaspoon vanilla

¾ cup walnuts or pecans,
   coarsely chopped


Mix dough. I use my hands. Press into mini muffing pan. Do not use papers. Spoon filling into each crust. Preheat oven to 350°. Bake for 20 minutes. Yield: 2 dozen tarts

THE LORD IS MY STRENGTH AND SONG,
and is become my salvation.

Psalm 118:14

# Fruit Top Cookies

**2 cups sucanat**

**1 cup butter, softened**

**2 eggs**

**4 cups fresh ground flour**

**1 teaspoon soda**

**4 Tablespoons milk**

**1 teaspoon vanilla**

Mix sucanat, butter, and eggs. Add remaining ingredients. Roll dough into little balls, about golf ball size or smaller, flatten slightly and poke a flat hole into the top with your thumb. Fill the hole with a dab of jam or thickened fruit or pie filling. Bake 375° for 10–13 minutes until done. Do not over bake.

*Note: These cookies are softer when stored in a cool place overnight, tightly covered.*

I WILL BLESS THE LORD AT ALL TIMES:
*his praise shall continually be in my mouth.*

Psalm 34:1

# Whole Wheat Pie Crust

3 cups fresh ground flour

1 teaspoon salt

1 ½ cups cold butter, cut in cubes

½ cup (4 ounces) cream cheese, cold,
   cut into cubes

4 Tablespoons cold water

Crumble all the ingredients together with your hands except water. When you have mixed it into consistent crumbs gradually add water. Roll crusts out on a well-floured counter, turning crusts over often as you roll. Small pies are easier to make. Enjoy and Experiment.

*Note: This is my only very successful all whole wheat pie crust recipe. Before this I had to use half white flour or (yes really) just bought them. With an "all or nothing" mind I guess I opted for nothing! Granted we do not eat desserts on a regular basis so it wasn't the fruit pies I missed so much, but I love chicken pies. Because of this I kept persevering and here are the results! A nourishing, delicious, flaky, pie crust.*

*Be completely humble and gentle;
be patient, bearing with
one another in love.*

Ephesians 4:2

# Cheesecake Cupcakes

3 (8 ounce) cream cheese, softened

5 eggs

¾ cup honey

2 teaspoons vanilla


  Topping:

1 cup sour cream

¼ cup honey

½ teaspoon vanilla


Preheat oven to 300°. Mix well and pour into paper-lined tiny muffin cups, about 2 tablespoonful in each. Bake 30–40 minutes. Remove from oven and top with 1 teaspoon topping on each. Dot with nuts, cherry, or a drop of jam. Bake 5 more minutes. Cool and refrigerate. Yield: 48 little tarts

*Note: Sometimes I use regular size cupcake tins as well.*

**Variations:**

*– You can make a delicious cheese cake with this same recipe. Just pour it into a crust, bake and refrigerate.*

# Tiny Chocolate Cherry Cheesecake

**Crust:**

1 cup flour

¼ cup sucanat

¼ cup cocoa

½ cup cold butter

2 Tablespoons water

**Filling:**

1 (8 ounce) cream cheese, softened

1 egg

¼ cup honey

1 teaspoon vanilla

Preheat oven at 325°. Combine all the crust ingredients, cutting in the cold butter, then add water last, tossing with a fork until dough forms a ball. Shape into 24 balls. Press dough into the bottom and sides of well greased miniature cupcake pans. Into each dough crust, put 1 tablespoon filling.

Bake 15-18 minutes. Cool 30 minutes before removing from pans. Put about 2 teaspoons of jam, pie filling or cherry on each cupcake.

# Ice Cream

2 Tablespoons plain gelatin

½ cup cold water

4 cups whole milk

1 cup sucanat or maple syrup

2 teaspoons vanilla

1 teaspoon salt

3 cups heavy cream

1 teaspoon stevia powder

Soak gelatin and water for 5 minutes. In a separate bowl mix rest of ingredients. Heat the gelatin mixture until boiling. Stirring constantly. Whisk in some of the milk mixture to cool it somewhat, then mix it all together. Churn in an ice cream maker according to the manual's instructions.

*Note: When using my own cream I use only 3 cups milk. This recipe keeps a better* consistency when frozen than the others I have tried. Of course, we seldom have leftovers to freeze.

*Variations:*

*– The variations are limited to your imagination! Use fruit or jams, crushed cookies, peanut butter, or whatever you dream up.*

# Chocolate Shoo-Fly Pie

Pudding:

2 Tablespoons organic cornstarch

2 cups sucanat

1 Tablespoon flour

3 Tablespoons cocoa

2 eggs

2 cups water

1 teaspoon vanilla

1 Tablespoon butter

Topping:

½ cup molasses

1 cup hot water

1 teaspoon vanilla

1 cup sucanat

½ cup butter

1 egg

¼ cup cocoa

1 teaspoon soda

¼ teaspoon salt

¼ teaspoon cinnamon

2 cups fresh ground flour

Mix pudding ingredients in a saucepan, cook until thick. Keep stirring it untill thick. Pour into three pie crusts. Combine topping ingredients. Pour over pudding mixture. Bake at 350° for 1 hour.

Cool and top with whipped cream if desired.

184

Cast thy burden upon the Lord,

and he shall sustain thee: he shall

**NEVER SUFFER THE RIGHTEOUS TO BE MOVED.**

Psalm 55:22

# Fruit Cobbler

4 cups fruit, fresh or frozen

½ cup maple syrup, honey, or
    coconut sugar, optional

½ cup butter, softened or melted

½ cup sucanat or coconut sugar

2 eggs

2 cups fresh ground flour

1 teaspoon soda

1 teaspoon baking powder

2 teaspoons cinnamon

1 cup milk or cream

Mix fruit and sweetener and put into a 9"x13" baking dish. In a mixing bowl, cream together butter, sweetener and eggs. Add flour, soda, baking powder, cinnamon and cream. Pour batter over fruit. Bake at 350° for 30–40 minutes or until golden brown. Serve warm. Great with milk, ice cream or whipped cream.

**Variations:**

*–Fruit variations: Strawberry Rhubarb, Peach, Blueberry, Apple and Cinnamon, Cherry, stone them first. Pie fillings work great for the fruit filling.*

But he was wounded for our transgressions,
he was bruised for our iniquities: the chastisement of our peace was upon him;
*and with his stripes we are healed.*

Isaiah 53:5

# Fruit Pizza

1 large egg

1 cup maple syrup or sucanat

1 cup butter, softened or melted

1 teaspoon vanilla

$2\frac{1}{4}$ cups flour

1 teaspoon baking powder

$\frac{1}{2}$ teaspoon salt

1 (8 ounce) cream cheese, softened

$\frac{1}{4}$ cup maple syrup

1 cup heavy cream, whipped

juice from 2 lemons & water to make 1 c.

$\frac{1}{4}$ to $\frac{1}{2}$ cup honey, maple syrup, or stevia

2 teaspoons organic cornstarch or tapioca starch

Cream together egg, maple syrup or sucanat, butter and vanilla. Add flour, baking powder and salt. Mix and pat onto a 12" round pizza pan. Bake 20–25 minutes at 350° until golden brown. Cool completely. Beat cream cheese. Add $\frac{1}{4}$ cup maple syrup. Whip heavy cream until soft peaks form. Add to cream cheese mixture. Spread over crust. Mix lemon juice and $\frac{1}{4}$ cup sweetener. Choose any fruit you want and arrange on pizza. Add starch to the juice and heat until thick. Keep stirred. Cool a bit and pour over fruit. Refrigerate.

*Tip: You can use canned pineapples and thicken this juice instead of using lemon juice. Add water to make 1 cup juice. Omit honey if desired.*

**Variations:**

— Fruit variations: sliced bananas, strawberries, pineapples, blueberries, cherries, pitted, small orange slices, kiwi.

Greater love has no one than this,
that he lay down
his life for his friends.

John 15:13

# Peanut Butter Bars

½ cup peanut butter

½ cup butter, softened

1 cup sucanat

2 eggs

2 teaspoons vanilla

1 cup fresh ground flour

1 teaspoon baking powder

¼ teaspoon salt

Topping:

½ cup coconut oil or butter

½ cup honey or maple syrup

¼ cup cocoa powder

Mix together peanut butter, butter, sucanat, eggs, and vanilla until creamy. Add flour, baking powder and salt. Put into a 9"x13" pan. Bake about 20–25 minutes at 350°. Cool slightly before adding topping. Melt together topping ingredients on stove top. Pour over slightly cooled bars.

*Note: This makes an excellent warm fudge topping for ice cream. It hardens as you pour it on the ice cream.*

# Pumpkin Pies

1 cup pumpkin puree

3 Tablespoons flour

1 ½ cup sucanat

½ teaspoon stevia powder

1 teaspoon salt

1 teaspoon cinnamon

½ teaspoon nutmeg

3 egg yolks

3 cups hot milk

Mix well, then beat the egg whites until stiff. Fold into the pumpkin mixture. Pour into two 8″ unbaked pie shells and bake at 350° for 50 minutes or until nicely browned and crusts are done.

HE WILL NOT SUFFER THY FOOT TO BE MOVED:
he that keepeth thee will not slumber.

Psalm 121:3

# Raspberry Mousse

¾ cup raspberry juice, concentrate

1 cup cold water

1 Tablespoon plain gelatin

1 (8 ounce) cream cheese, softened

½ cup honey or maple syrup

stevia, if desired

2 cups whipped cream

Soak gelatin in water, about 5 minutes. Heat until boiling. Be careful, keep it stirred so it doesn't burn or boil over. In a separate bowl whisk the cream cheese until smooth. Gradually add raspberry juice, honey, and the gelatin mixture. Gently fold whipped cream into raspberry mixture. Refrigerate.

Note: I can raspberry juice in the summer by cooking raspberries and water, then straining. Welch has frozen raspberry concentrate as well. If using fresh, raw cream I need to add ½ Tablespoon more gelatin, depending on the consistency of the cream.

*The name of the Lord is a strong tower:*
the righteous runneth into it, and is safe.
Proverbs 18:10

# Homemaker Helps

## Idealism & Reality

Although it is my desire to, I do not make all my own pastas, crackers, nut butters, sauces, cheeses, and condiments. Maybe someday! But right now I am a busy mother of seven. Realistically, there is no way I can do all this, have a garden, homeschool, sew, and teach my children well in the ways of the Lord, and be a helpful wife to my man! I am content in making what I have time for.

If you were to learn only one thing from me let it be this — consider your priorities and let nothing rob you from these. First, love the Lord, serve your husband and raise your children to love and follow Jesus, and as you're doing all these important things then make nourishing foods with your children and teach them "why" and "how!"

Seek ye first the Kingdom of God,

and his righteousness;

AND ALL THESE THINGS

shall be added unto you.

Matthew 6:33.

# Beverages

# Stevia Sweetened Lemonade

1 cup freshly squeezed lemon juice

½–1 teaspoon stevia powder

6 cups water

maple syrup, optional

*Variatons:*

*– For strawberry Lemonade: Add about 15–20 strawberries blended in 1 cup water. If you want a strawberry lemonade without seeds you can pour it through a sieve.*

Come unto me, all ye that labour and are heavy laden, and I will give you rest.

**TAKE MY YOKE UPON YOU, AND LEARN OF ME;**

for I am meek and lowly in heart: and ye shall find rest unto your souls.

For my yoke is easy, and my burden is light.

Matthew 11:28-30

199

# Smoothies

1 ½ quarts kefir or yogurt

1 cup fresh cream

2–3 cup fresh fruit or berries

2 bananas

2 Tablespoons honey

stevia, if desired

juice of 1 orange, optional

Combine ingredients and blend in blender and serve. A refreshing summer treat. Kefir is very easy to make. If your kefir gets too strong you'll want to use less than 1 ½ quarts. Adjust fruit to taste.

### Variations:

– If we have leftover smoothie (If!). I soak a tablespoon or 2 of beef gelatin in cold water then heat it to boiling. Add to smoothie and blend quickly. Refrigerate in a bowl and you have a yummy Jell-O.

Trust in the Lord with all thine heart;
*and lean not unto thine own understanding.*
In all thy ways acknowledge him, and he shall direct thy paths.
Proverbs 3:5-6

# Chocolate Milk Mix

1 ½ cups water

2 ½ cups coconut sugar or sucanat, more
if you prefer a sweet mix

1 ½ cups cocoa

2 teaspoons vanilla

stevia, optional


In a saucepan dissolve water and sweetener.
Add cocoa and stevia. Mix until smooth.
Keep refrigerated. Mix with milk as desired.

### Variations:

– Sometimes I use honey or maple syrup.

AND THE LORD, HE IT IS THAT DOTH GO BEFORE THEE;
*he will be with thee, he will not fail thee, neither forsake thee:*
fear not, neither be dismayed.

Deuteronomy 31:8

# Homemaker Helps

# Index

# Index

## Breakfast

## Breads & Salads

## Soups & Sandwiches

Index

# Beverages